A Cat

RIVERHEAD
BOOKS
New York

A Cat

LEONARD MICHAELS

Illustrations by Frances Lerner

Riverhead Books
Published by The Berkley Publishing Group
200 Madison Avenue
New York, New York 10016

Copyright © 1995 by Leonard Michaels
Book design by Claire Naylon Vaccaro
Cover design by Isabella Fasciano
Cover illustration © 1995 by Frances Lerner

Riverhead hardcover edition: October 1995
First Riverhead trade paperback edition: November 1996
Riverhead trade paperback ISBN: 1-57322-566-5

The Putnam Berkley World Wide Web site address is
http://www.berkley.com/berkley

The Library of Congress has catalogued the Riverhead
hardcover edition as follows:

Michaels, Leonard, date.
    A cat / by Leonard Michaels ; illustrations by Frances Lerner.
        p.   cm.
    ISBN 1-57322-013-2
    1. Cats—Miscellanea. 1. Title.
    SF445.5.M52   1995   94-25257 CIP
    636.8—dc20

Printed in the United States of America

10   9   8   7   6   5   4   3   2   1

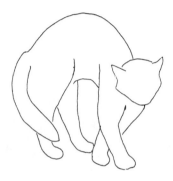

A Cat

A cat is content to be a cat.

A cat is not owned by anybody.

Some animals are secretive; some are shy. A cat is private.

A cat would sooner die than pee in public.

A cat is beautiful, and no cat is far more appealing than most. Cole Porter wouldn't have written, "Though your face is charming, it's the wrong face," about a cat.

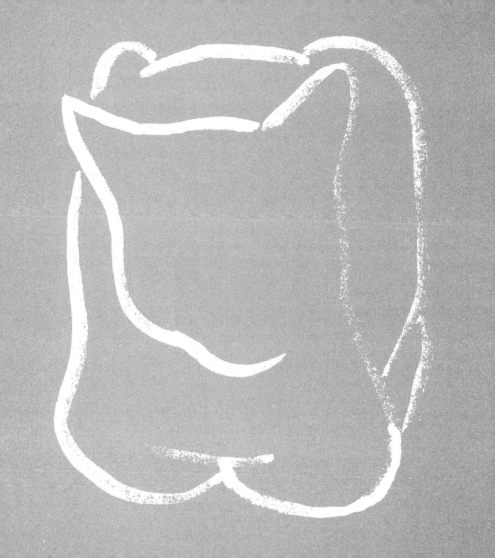

A cat sees in black and white. Like a character in a forties movie, it seems born to wear a tuxedo or evening gown, and it behaves elegantly.

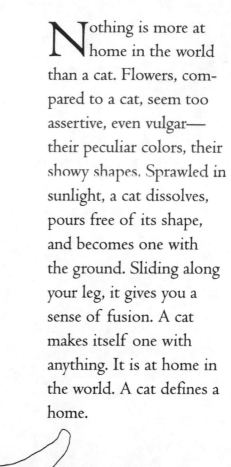

Nothing is more at home in the world than a cat. Flowers, compared to a cat, seem too assertive, even vulgar— their peculiar colors, their showy shapes. Sprawled in sunlight, a cat dissolves, pours free of its shape, and becomes one with the ground. Sliding along your leg, it gives you a sense of fusion. A cat makes itself one with anything. It is at home in the world. A cat defines a home.

A cat weighs about as much as a baby, and it sleeps most of the day; but if a cat were fifteen pounds heavier, it wouldn't seem cute, and it could tear your throat out.

Face-to-face with a cat, you see almost no mouth. Its expression is unforthcoming, uncommunicative. Eyes and ears. A tiny, cool, exquisite nose. Without much mouth, the face seems uninterested in eating, and the eyes seem large and salient, as though a cat wants only to observe, to know things. A cat's whiskers, like exquisite antennae, read the airiest messages.

A cat licks its hand to wash its face and to wash behind its ears, and it has a good idea of how big it is and what its body can do. An actor might learn much by studying a cat. The first lesson would be in poise and self-possession. The next would be what weight to give statements of feeling, from the most pitiful cry to the most piercing and unearthly wail. Hardest to learn from a cat is how not to appear to be acting.

A cat doesn't look at itself when you hold it up to a mirror. It acts as if nothing appeared in the glass. That's because a cat believes it is invisible. A cat has to believe this, because, when stalking, it has to be invisible in the eyes of its prey. To be a cat you must be invisible and very real at the same time. Worshippers believe this of God.

The soul of another is a dark forest"
sounds like what a cat might say,
but it comes from a story by Chekhov.

A cat imagines things about you, nothing you can know for sure.

When a cat shuts its eyes, you disappear.

You look at a cat, and it looks at you. You have the scary idea that a cat is a kind of person. You look more carefully and let the cat's eyes tell you what it sees. It sees you are a kind of cat.

A cat always looks into your eyes, as if it knows that you see it with your eyes. As if it knows? What a mad idea. A cat doesn't even know it has eyes, let alone know that it is seeing you with its eyes. And yet it knows, it knows.

A cat comes and goes. Its interests are independent of yours, though it may want to sleep with you, or climb into your lap and sit there for a while. But it is unlikely to go for a walk with you, as will a dog. In a cat's social life, you are marginal unless it wants attention. To get your attention it claws the furniture, shredding the wooden leg of a table or the fabric of a couch and then tearing out the stuffing. This can make a person hysterical, which is an extremely intense show of attention.

There are times when you feel so bad you can't say anything, but even crying your eyes out you can sit with a cat in your lap.

When you see a cat lying in a box or cage, you don't want to reach in and lift it out. You want to slide in beside the cat.

While stroking a cat, you may see it twist and writhe with pleasure, and feel it purr and vibrate beneath your hand, and you may find yourself stroking it more vigorously, and kneading its muscles, giving it more pleasure and more pleasure and then, in a blur of needle teeth, it nips your hand. Between pleasure and aggression, there is a flash point.

The tail of a cat lashes, curls, and swishes slowly. It stands straight up. It vibrates. It blooms before battle and looks three times thicker. It is a flag of feelings—courage, shame, pleasure, fear. It can become the hook of a sickle, or a shepherd's crook, or a rod, or a plume, or an S, and it can press down to seal a cat's heinie. It is the poetry and prose of a cat. When a cat is thoughtful, the tail moves like a part of the mind. It is a moody river, a smokey flow. It is a sentence, the material shape of an idea. It is an announcement, a revelation, and an artistic gesture, beautiful even if only to express boredom.

A cat's tail never drags on the ground as does the train of a wedding dress, or some other formal gown that we wear on ritual occasions, whether solemn or gay, to remember our animal roots. When a woman catches up the train of a gown and sweeps it to one side or the other, you see instantly that she is flaunting her tail.

A cat's head points to the future, and its tail, like another head, points back to the past. The tail-head is skinnier than the head in front, and of course it has no eyes, ears, or mouth. It isn't useful, except as a proud expression of the ancient history of cats, a gorgeous memory of life in the trees. Too bad we lost our tail, since nothing is sexier-looking. Think of the women on magazine covers, coyly hiding their private parts. Oh, let the truth be seen. Compared to a cat, we're made of nothing but practical parts, and a posterior without posterity.

As with a work of art, you never completely understand a cat. This is true of other things, too, but their mystery is seldom haunting, and we feel no desire to possess them. People have rushed into a burning house, risking their lives, to save a painting or a cat.

Every feeling, from eery dread to unashamed love, can be involved with a cat. Of all animals only a cat makes you wonder what it feels about us.

When a cat is much offended, it hisses, a sound of ferocity and moral indignation. The sound is frightening, though you don't fear any harm a cat can do to you. You fear its feelings.

A cat knows what happens to you after you die.

A cat will do a certain thing five times, but if you want it done six times, it won't do it—until you forget and look away.

Touch it wrong, or at the wrong moment, and a cat slips out of reach. It doesn't want to be touched. But catch it anyway and a cat goes limp in your arms. It wants to be touched.

When your hand strokes its back, a cat feels its own beautiful lines. It purrs. It loves the feeling—not your hand—the feeling of itself.

When it comes to loneliness, a cat is excellent company. It is a lonely animal. It understands what you feel. A dog also understands, but it makes such a big deal of being there for you, bumping against you, flopping about your feet, licking your face. It keeps saying, "Here I am." Your loneliness then seems lugubrious. A cat will just be, suffering with you in philosophical silence.

With a dog in the house, you imagine yourself protected against intruders and you sleep better. With a cat in the bed, you don't think about intruders. You feel innocent, and it seems no harm will come. A cat can't protect you against intruders, only against dreams, the terrors within.

Not simply another species,
a cat belongs to an order
of being different from dogs.

Dogs tend to look like their masters,
but this is never true of a cat. A
cat is a highly particular creature.

A cat is aristocratic, as comfortable in a castle as in a humble home, as self-reliant in fields and forests as in a street.

Fluid and quick, a cat also
undulates like a caterpillar,
the spine rising and falling
in waves.

To be quick as a cat you must not think.

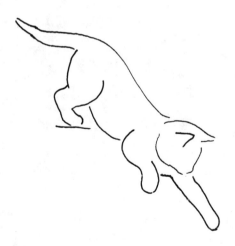

Compared to a cat we're big, slow, blundering figures. When we lie down, our gross, earthen nature must make us appear something like rocks and trees to a cat. Therefore, it feels free to walk on us.

A cat's fury, like a meteor hissing across the night sky, is gone before you take it in. Then there is only darkness. The privacy of a cat.

Stalking prey, a cat often stretches full length and crouches low to the ground, and the tip of its tail swishes slowly, nervously. That's when it looks like a man sighting down a cue stick, shooting pool.

When a cat eats it gobbles, crouched, bunched up as if to spring away from danger at any moment. Its tail lies flat along the floor, the tip curved slightly to the left or right, the direction of flight.

The smoothness and softness and warmth of a cat is contradicted by its tongue, which is like the surface of a rasp.

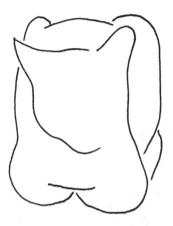

Some believe a cat will suck the breath out of a baby. This isn't true, but when you wake up with a cat sitting on your chest, staring into your face and breathing your air, you understand why some believe it.

A cat bunched up and sleepy is like a cumulous cloud. Stretched out on its side, flat along the ground, it is like a stratus cloud. Clouds piled up high are like a great council of cats in silent meditation.

A cat talks to another cat the way we hum to a tuning fork.

A cats' chorus is their way of feeling with one another, and feeling less isolated among humans.

The silence of a cat makes the world unreal.

A stream of thought and dreamy images, for which no words exist, flows endlessly along the nerves of a cat.

A cat is dreamy. It loves the night, the adventurous darkness where it swims like a fish in oil.

Odysseus left home for twenty years. A cat leaves only for a night, but night after night it returns like Odysseus, with memories of war and love.

There is a cat place in this world, though not anywhere you can point to. It is a place of pure sensation that has very little to do with words. When you say, "Come here," a cat looks everywhere but at you. It hates the sensation of words invading the cat place, and won't come.

When a cat decides—entirely on its own—to come to you, it is moved entirely from within. A cat does not feel compelled to do anything by convention or custom or guilt, so its decision is freely made, natural, and profound. It offers you truly personal recognition, a pleasure otherwise received only from a lover, though never so pure and trustworthy.

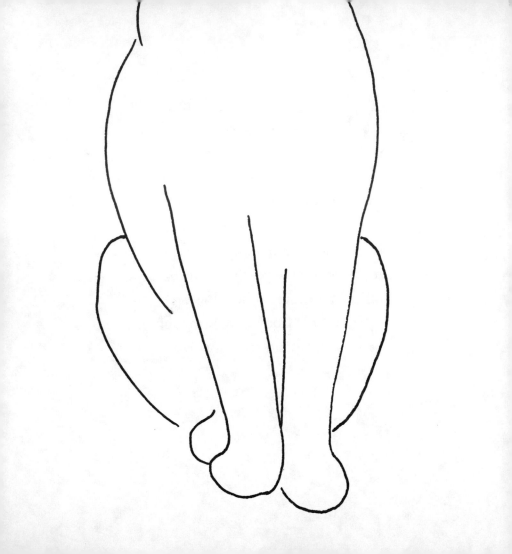

The word "cat" is very old. Nobody knows where it comes from. The exact origin of the cat itself is also unknown. A cat reminds us that much in this world remains unknown.

A cat walking across a room is a dramatic occasion, weary, painfully slow, or stiff-legged and tense with apprehension. Then it stops, looks back the way it came, torn by questions about where it really wants to go.

It's hard to sneak up on a cat, unless you walk on air.

A cat's brain is only about the size of a pecan. But if a closet door is left slightly open, a cat will use its little hand to pull it open further and then slip inside. This might not seem like much, and yet a cat makes an impression of quiet wisdom.

If you think long enough about what you see in a cat, you begin to suppose you will understand everything, but its eyes tell you there is nothing to understand, there is only life.

When it's hungry or needs attention, a cat nags you. Otherwise, it is reserved and makes an impression of dignity, stillness, and poise. Poised to fight, a cat sits still as a stone, and, before you see it move, it moved. From stillness to bloody claws. "Quick as a cat," you say, for it must be compared only to itself.

In the motion of a cat you see paws, tail, ears, nose, spine, and belly flow like words in a sentence. Below the words, the play of a cat's muscles is a grammatical exercise.

A cat may look at a king," says Alice. It is enough to say. It makes sense, and yet you want something more. You want to say it isn't enough for us to look at a cat.

Looking at a cat, like looking at clouds or stars or the ocean, makes it difficult to believe there is nothing miraculous in this world.

A neurotic cat is not so sweet as others, not so easily lovable. It is more human than a cat should be.

P eople have noticed that a cat can love them, but they don't then remember that a cat isn't rational. So irrational, it seems almost human.

People wonder how a cat resembles them psychologically. A cat wonders similarly about people.

It isn't that a cat has nothing to say, but it wouldn't want to write a poem or a book or anything. In contrast, Virginia Woolf felt the day had been wasted if she didn't write in her diary. For a cat, just to live is splendid.

The expression "Don't get your back up" was inspired by a cat, and so are words like "catcall," "catwalk," "cat's-eye," "cattail," "cat's-paw," "catty," "catbird," "catfish." Catwords make a catalogue.

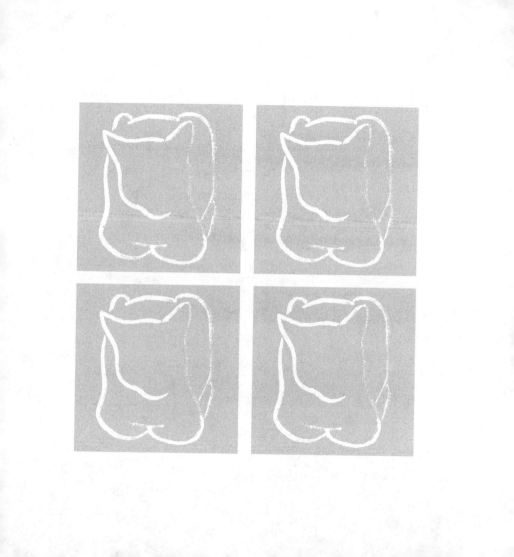

The strings of a violin, called "catgut," have nothing to do with cats, but a violin has eyes, teeth, and a tail, and is passionately aroused when stroked. A cat without legs.

We say, "You struck a chord," or "There was a certain note in your voice." Everything a cat says is musical. Music is much older than talk. The first words were notes. The first sentence was a song. Our deepest feelings are expressed only as music.

You might suppose the word "catch," for which there are many meanings, comes from the ancient word "cat."

When threatening to fight, cats whine at each other, a blood-curdling sound, shrill with miserable lamentation. They foresee the ghastly lacerations they will inflict and suffer, and already regret them. Suddenly the whining stops. There is an eery silence, wherein lie inexpressible terrors, as each cat wishes the other would go away.

A cat spends much time alone thinking about itself and knows its darkest desires. Naturally, it is mistrustful of other cats.

A cat is susceptible to certain low emotions, like jealousy. Nobody is perfect.

Much that is meaningful between you and a cat transpires in silence. It isn't different between people.

Something tragic in the gaze of a cat makes you want to apologize. You wonder what you did wrong. You fed the cat, but it gazes at you in that tragic way. You stroked the cat and heard it purring, but it gazes at you that tragic way and gives you no credit for trying.

A cat's ears are triangles. Another two triangles are formed by lines dropping from its brow down either side of its nose and then slanted back up past the outside corners of its eyes. Thus, in the shape of its ears and the shape enclosing its eyes, you see four triangles. Fit them together and you have a square. The square overlaps the circle which is the cat's face. Square, circle, triangle—basic to the construction of the world—are in the face of a cat.

A cat may love you, but unlike people it can't say, "I love you like a million dollars," or "I love you so much I want to eat you up," or "I'd die for you." With its little soul, a cat loves you as much as it can without insisting, without risk to you of disappointment, humiliation, or grief.

A cat smells, listens, looks, touches, tastes, and thus, in sensations alone, it discovers meaning. If you lie on the floor beside a cat, it will examine you. No matter how stale, flat, and unprofitable you are to others, you will be meaningful to a cat.

A cat has a large repertoire of gestures. Some are peculiar to its twitching ears, brilliant eyes, kneading paws, swishing tail, and shivery fur. Some are peculiar to its cameling back, its stretching legs, its tipping-turning head. A cat is a collection of electrical and particular peculiarities. When its eyes squeeze sleepily shut, many teeny inner cats become quiet and go to sleep.

A cat draws a cloak of moody silence about itself and retreats within to a secret auditorium, where a parliament of inner cats make speeches and elect leaders.

A cat lives mainly by its instincts. If it makes a mistake in judgment, it remains dignified and never looks like a fool.

A cat demands respect for the distance between itself and other creatures, but anytime it likes it smears its face against you, leaps into your lap or into your bed, and sleeps with you. It shows no respect for distance. This is paradoxical and self-contradictory, but a cat isn't worried about logic. From a certain point of view, such god-like arrogance demonstrates enlightenment, the achievement of nirvana.

Watch a cat closely for a long time and you will begin to wonder if it isn't conscious of being watched, playing a role, pretending to be a cat.

People say, "I like dogs," a remark that includes, in a broad and affectionate sweep, dachshund, wolfhound, Chihuahua, poodle, pit bull, and others. There is no essential, basic dog, and that's what people like—dogs—an adorable plurality, a fantastic multiplicity. But there is an essential cat—lonely, wild, secretive, sensual—from whom no cat diverges very far in shape or character. However a cat looks or behaves, it is what it is, a small and intensely serious being, a cat.

A cat never has nothing to do. It stretches, rubs its cheeks and ribs against furniture, humps its back, claws wood, and looks out the window. Even when it's asleep, a cat's ears swivel about, listening to what's happening in its territory. Sometimes—but not often—a cat may watch television with you, but mainly it doesn't waste its life with entertainment.

Dogs, birds, and ferrets can be trained to hunt. A cat refuses to be trained. Superb hunter, it will not enslave its genius for a person. However, if a cat loves you, it may bring you a kill, warm and bleeding, and drop it on the living-room rug where you can't fail to see it, or drop it beside your bedroom slippers so that, first thing in the morning, you can step on it. A cat's gift—warm, soft, wet kiss against the bottom of your naked foot—leaves a red blotch, like lipstick.

If you say, "A cat is blind to itself in a mirror," someone else says, "No, that isn't true. I've seen kittens strike at their reflections," or "My cat was once surprised by its reflection, and arched its back." Hardly anything you say about a cat fails to elicit contradiction, or happy agreement, or anecdotes. Cat-conversations, full of amazed and intimate revelations, aren't like the way we talk about dogs.

A cat's mouth seems hidden, nearly invisible. Therefore its eyes are especially telling, so clear and luminous. But a hidden mouth suggests mystery, the mystery of identity with an erotic charge, as in the face of a man whose moustache obscures his mouth, or a woman who peers above a veil. These eyes are messengers who say: "You don't know me." We learned the hidden-mouth look, with its mixture of invitation and taboo, from a cat.

A cat can move so slowly that it seems not to move at all, or somehow to move by not moving, which is a metaphysical feat, crucial to stalking prey. A Buddhist asks: "Which is moving, the flag or the wind?" You might ask: "Which is moving, the cat or the world?"

The ears of a cat swivel in all directions, even backwards. Its eyes, nose, and whiskers are keenly sensitive, and its paws detect vibrations of the earth made by footsteps, or movements of continental plates, or the gravitational pull of the moon. It knows a great deal. Nothing can easily surprise a cat, but it cannot know how we make it live in writing or drawing, how we take it into our minds for the pleasure of thinking about a cat.

When you are packing clothes in a suitcase, your cat will come sit on the clothes. It assumes you will include it on your trip. This can seem absurd and funny. You laugh and go out the door. But when you return, your cat acts haughtily, as if it doesn't care that you're home, as if it hardly knows you. In your relation to a cat there is a sweetness that isn't absurd. It is more heartbreaking than funny.

The author of books including the novel *The Men's Club* and the fictional memoir *Sylvia*, **Leonard Michaels** has also written stories and essays that have appeared in *Prize Stories: The O. Henry Awards*, *The Best American Short Stories*, and *The Best American Essays*. He has received a Guggenheim Fellowship and an award from the American Academy and Institute of Arts and Letters, and his writing has been nominated for the National Book Award and the National Book Critics Circle Award. He lives in the San Francisco Bay area.